6-12 months

- ♥ SEND AN ENGAGEMENT GIFT TO THE BRIDE
- ♥ HELP THE BRIDE TO SELECT THE VENUE
- ♥ JOIN THE BRIDE DURING DRESS SHOPPING
- ♥ HELP LOOK FOR THE BRIDESMAID DRESSES
- ♥ GET IN TOUCH WITH THE BRIDESMAIDS AND PLAN A MEETING TO GET TO KNOW EACH OTHER
- ♥ BRAINSTORM BRIDAL SHOWER/BACHELORETTE PARTY IDEAS

4-6 months

- ♥ PURCHASE DRESSES
- ♥ START PLANNING BRIDAL SHOWER/BACHELORETTE PARTY
- ♥ HELP THE BRIDE ADDRESS INVITES
- ♥ BOOK FLIGHTS AND HOTEL (IF NECESSARY)

3-4 months

- ♥ SCHEDULE ALTERATION APPOINTMENTS FOR DRESSES
- ♥ PURCHASE SHOES, ACCESSORIES AND JEWELRY

2-3 months

- ♥ THROW BRIDAL PARTY (SEE PLANNER)
- ♥ COORDINATE BRIDESMAIDS HAIR AND MAKEUP
- ♥ SCHEDULE HAIR, MAKEUP AND NAILS APPOINTMENT
- ♥ LOOK FOR A WEDDING GIFT

1-2 months

- ♥ THROW BACHELORETTE PARTY (SEE PLANNER)
- ♥ WRITE MAID OF HONOR SPEECH (SEE WEDDING TOAST)
- ♥ HELP THE BRIDE WITH ERRANDS

2-4 weeks

- ♥ PACK A BRIDAL EMERGENCY PACK (SEE EXAMPLE LIST)
- ♥ DOUBLE CHECK ALL ARRANGEMENTS

1 weeks

- ♥ SUPPORT THE BRIDE EMOTIONALLY
- ♥ MAKE SURE THAT THE BRIDESMAIDS HAVE ALL THE INFORMATION THEY NEED

1 day before the wedding

- ♥ ATTEND WEDDING REHEARSAL AND DINNER
- ♥ LAYOUT CLOTHING

wedding day

- ♥ HAIR APPOINTMENT AT _____
- ♥ MAKEUP APPOINTMENT AT _____
- ♥ NAILS APPOINTMENT AT _____
- ♥ KEEP TRACK OF RINGS
- ♥ SEE THE BRIDE AT _____
- ♥ TIME OF PHOTO SHOOT _____
- ♥ NAILS APPOINTMENT AT _____
- ♥ KEEP TRACK OF RINGS
- ♥ GIVE YOUR SPEECH

_____

_____

_____

_____

_____

_____

_____

_____

bridal shower

Date

Venue: _____

Contact details: _____

_____

_____

plan

To-do:

Time	Agenda

❤ _____

❤ _____

❤ _____

❤ _____

❤ _____

❤ _____

❤ _____

❤ _____

❤ _____

❤ _____

❤ _____

❤ _____

❤ _____

❤ _____

Food and drinks

Games

>>> _____

>>> _____

>>> _____

>>> _____

>>> _____

>>> _____

>>> _____

>>> _____

>>> _____

>>> _____

Decorations

>>> _____

>>> _____

>>> _____

>>> _____

guestlist

Name and Contact	RSVP

bridal shower budget

Name and	Budget	Deposit	Balance/due	Total spend
Venue				
Catering				
Beverages				
Alcohol				
Staff				
Cake				
Tableware equipment hire				
Games				
Table decorations				
Flowers				
Apparel				

bachelorette party

Date

Venue:_____

Contact details:_____

_____

_____

plan

Time	Agenda

To-do:

- ❤ _____
- ❤ _____
- ❤ _____
- ❤ _____
- ❤ _____
- ❤ _____
- ❤ _____
- ❤ _____
- ❤ _____
- ❤ _____
- ❤ _____
- ❤ _____
- ❤ _____
- ❤ _____
- ❤ _____

Food and drinks

Games

>>> _____

>>> _____

>>> _____

>>> _____

>>> _____

>>> _____

>>> _____

>>> _____

>>> _____

>>> _____

>>> _____

>>> _____

>>> _____

>>> _____

>>> _____

Decorations

guestlist

Name and Contact	RSVP

Notes_____

_____

_____

_____

_____

_____

_____

_____

_____

_____

_____

bachelorette party budget

Name and	Budget	Deposit	Balance/due	Total spend
Venue				
Catering				
Beverages				
Alcohol				
Staff				
Cake				
Tableware equipment hire				
Games				
Table decorations				
Flowers				
Apparel				

maid of honor attire

dress

Shop _____

Contact details _____

_____

Order date _____ Fitting date _____

Dress details _____

Pick up date

_____

_____

shoes and accessories

Item	Details	Received

beauty

hair

Salon _____

Contact details _____

_____

Stylist _____

Style _____

Deposit _____ Total _____

makeup

Salon _____

Contact details _____

_____

Artist _____

Style _____

Deposit _____ Total _____

nails

Salon _____

Contact details _____

_____

Artist _____

Style _____

Deposit _____ Total _____

bridesmaid attire

dresses

Shop _____

Contact details _____

_____

Order date _____ Fitting date _____

Notes _____

_____

_____

_____

Pick up date

Size	Color	Who is wearing it?	Notes

shoes and accessories

Item	Details	Received

weddings toast

START PLANNING YOUR SPEECH ONE OR TWO MONTHS IN ADVANCE. LET A FRIEND PROOFREAD IT.

avoid

- DO NOT MENTION EX-BOYFRIENDS OR EX-HUSBANDS
- REMEMBER THAT BOTH FAMILIES ARE THERE, DO NOT BRING UP VERY EMBARRASSING STORIES
- DO NOT USE SWEAR WORDS

include in your toast

- HOW YOU KNOW THE BRIDE
- FUNNY STORIES THAT ARE NOT EMBARRASSING
- A SENTIMENTAL STORY FROM THE PAST
- A STORY ABOUT THE COUPLE: HOW THEY MET, HOW THEIR RELATIONSHIP BLOSSOMED OR WHAT MAKES THEM A PERFECT COUPLE
- BEST WISHES FOR THE COUPLE
- INVITE THE GUESTS TO RAISE THEIR GLASS

wedding toast

Introduce yourself

Humor/time for a pun

A story about the bride

Say something sweet about the groom

The couple

Humor/time for a pun

Toast

wedding emergency kit

makeup

- COTTON SWABS
- DEODORANT
- BABY WIPES
- TOOTHPASTE
- TOOTHBRUSH
- PERFUME
- MAKEUP REMOVER
- FOUNDATION
- POWDER
- EYELINER
- EYEBROW PENCIL
- LIPSTICK
- MASCARA
- LOTION
- BABY POWDER
- NAIL POLISH
- NAIL FILER

hair

- HAIRSPRAY
- BOBBY PINS
- COMB

miscellaneou

- TAMPONS AND PADS
- SNACKS
- TISSUES
- WATER
- NEEDLE AND THREAD
- LINT ROLLER
- RAZORS
- MEDICINES
- PAINKILLERS
- BUG SPRAY
- SUNSCREEN
- PHONE CHARGER
- CASH
- DRINKING STRAW
- HEM TAPE
- BLISTER REPAIR
- SMALL SCISSORS

week _____

Priorities

-
-
-

Notes

....

....

....

....

....

....

....

Appointments

_____

_____

_____

_____

_____

_____

_____

_____

Monday

Tuesday

Wednesday

Thursday

Friday

Saturday

Sunday

week _____

Priorities

-
-
-

Notes

Appointments

Monday
Tuesday
Wednesday
Thursday
Friday
Saturday
Sunday

week _____

Priorities

-
-
-

Notes

Appointments

Monday

Tuesday

Wednesday

Thursday

Friday

Saturday

Sunday

week _____

Priorities

-
-
-

Notes

Appointments

| Monday |
| Tuesday |
| Wednesday |
| Thursday |
| Friday |
| Saturday |
| Sunday |

Month of _____

Monday	Tuesday	Wednesday	Thursday

Friday	Saturday	Sunday	Notes

week _____

Priorities

-
-
-

Notes
....
....
....
....
....
....
....
....

Appointments
_____
_____
_____
_____
_____
_____
_____
_____

Monday

Tuesday

Wednesday

Thursday

Friday

Saturday

Sunday

week _____

Priorities

-
-
-

Notes

....
....
....
....
....
....
....

Appointments

| Monday |
| Tuesday |
| Wednesday |
| Thursday |
| Friday |
| Saturday |
| Sunday |

week _____

Priorities

-
-
-

Notes

....
....
....
....
....
....
....

Appointments

_____
_____
_____
_____
_____
_____
_____

Monday

Tuesday

Wednesday

Thursday

Friday

Saturday

Sunday

week _____

Priorities

-
-
-

Notes

Appointments

_____
_____
_____
_____
_____
_____
_____
_____

| Monday |
| Tuesday |
| Wednesday |
| Thursday |
| Friday |
| Saturday |
| Sunday |

Month of _____

Monday	Tuesday	Wednesday	Thursday

Friday	Saturday	Sunday	Notes

week _____

Priorities

-
-
-

Notes

....
....
....
....
....
....
....

Appointments

_____
_____
_____
_____
_____
_____
_____

Monday

Tuesday

Wednesday

Thursday

Friday

Saturday

Sunday

week _____

Priorities

-
-
-

Notes

Appointments

| Monday |
| Tuesday |
| Wednesday |
| Thursday |
| Friday |
| Saturday |
| Sunday |

week _____

Priorities

-
-
-

Notes
....
....
....
....
....
....
....

Appointments
_____
_____
_____
_____
_____
_____
_____
_____

Monday

Tuesday

Wednesday

Thursday

Friday

Saturday

Sunday

week _____

Priorities

-
-
-

Notes

Appointments

| Monday |
| Tuesday |
| Wednesday |
| Thursday |
| Friday |
| Saturday |
| Sunday |

Month of _____

Monday	Tuesday	Wednesday	Thursday

Friday	Saturday	Sunday	Notes

week _____

Priorities

-
-
-

Notes
....
....
....
....
....
....
....
....

Appointments
_____
_____
_____
_____
_____
_____
_____
_____

Monday

Tuesday

Wednesday

Thursday

Friday

Saturday

Sunday

week _____

Priorities

-
-
-

Notes

Appointments

Monday

Tuesday

Wednesday

Thursday

Friday

Saturday

Sunday

week _____

Priorities

-
-
-

Notes

....
....
....
....
....
....
....

Appointments

Monday

Tuesday

Wednesday

Thursday

Friday

Saturday

Sunday

week _____

Priorities

-
-
-

Notes

Appointments

| Monday |
| Tuesday |
| Wednesday |
| Thursday |
| Friday |
| Saturday |
| Sunday |

Month of _____

Monday	Tuesday	Wednesday	Thursday

Friday	Saturday	Sunday	Notes

week _____

Priorities

-
-
-

Notes

....
....
....
....
....
....
....
....

Appointments

_____
_____
_____
_____
_____
_____
_____
_____

Monday

Tuesday

Wednesday

Thursday

Friday

Saturday

Sunday

week _____

Priorities

-
-
-

Notes

Appointments

Monday

Tuesday

Wednesday

Thursday

Friday

Saturday

Sunday

week _____

Priorities

-
-
-

Notes

....
....
....
....
....
....
....
....

Appointments

_____
_____
_____
_____
_____
_____
_____
_____

Monday

Tuesday

Wednesday

Thursday

Friday

Saturday

Sunday

week _____

Priorities

-
-
-

Notes

Appointments

| Monday |
| Tuesday |
| Wednesday |
| Thursday |
| Friday |
| Saturday |
| Sunday |

Month of _____

Monday	Tuesday	Wednesday	Thursday

Friday	Saturday	Sunday	Notes

week _____

Priorities

-
-
-

Notes

....

....

....

....

....

....

....

Appointments

_____

_____

_____

_____

_____

_____

_____

Monday

Tuesday

Wednesday

Thursday

Friday

Saturday

Sunday

week _____

Priorities

-
-
-

Notes

Appointments

Monday

Tuesday

Wednesday

Thursday

Friday

Saturday

Sunday

week _____

Priorities

-
-
-

Notes
....
....
....
....
....
....
....
....

Appointments
_____
_____
_____
_____
_____
_____
_____

Monday

Tuesday

Wednesday

Thursday

Friday

Saturday

Sunday

week _____

Priorities

-
-
-

Notes

Appointments

| Monday |
| Tuesday |
| Wednesday |
| Thursday |
| Friday |
| Saturday |
| Sunday |

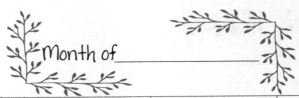

Month of_____

Monday	Tuesday	Wednesday	Thursday

Friday	Saturday	Sunday	Notes

week _____

Priorities

-
-
-

Notes

....
....
....
....
....
....
....
....

Appointments

_____
_____
_____
_____
_____
_____
_____
_____

Monday

Tuesday

Wednesday

Thursday

Friday

Saturday

Sunday

week _____

Priorities

-
-
-

Notes

....
....
....
....
....
....
....

Appointments

_____
_____
_____
_____
_____
_____
_____
_____

Monday
Tuesday
Wednesday
Thursday
Friday
Saturday
Sunday

week _____

Priorities

-
-
-

Notes

....
....
....
....
....
....
....

Appointments

_____
_____
_____
_____
_____
_____
_____

Monday

Tuesday

Wednesday

Thursday

Friday

Saturday

Sunday

week _____

Priorities

-
-
-

Notes

Appointments

Monday

Tuesday

Wednesday

Thursday

Friday

Saturday

Sunday

Month of_____

Monday	Tuesday	Wednesday	Thursday

Friday	Saturday	Sunday	Notes

week _____

Priorities

-
-
-

Notes

Appointments

Monday

Tuesday

Wednesday

Thursday

Friday

Saturday

Sunday

week _____

Priorities

-
-
-

Notes

....

....

....

....

....

....

....

Appointments

_____

_____

_____

_____

_____

_____

_____

_____

Monday
Tuesday
Wednesday
Thursday
Friday
Saturday
Sunday

week _____

Priorities

-
-
-

Notes

....
....
....
....
....
....
....

Appointments

_____
_____
_____
_____
_____
_____
_____
_____

Monday

Tuesday

Wednesday

Thursday

Friday

Saturday

Sunday

week _____

Priorities

-
-
-

Notes

....
....
....
....
....
....
....
....

Appointments

_____
_____
_____
_____
_____
_____
_____
_____
_____

| Monday |
| Tuesday |
| Wednesday |
| Thursday |
| Friday |
| Saturday |
| Sunday |

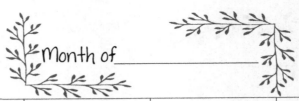

Month of_____

Monday	Tuesday	Wednesday	Thursday

Friday	Saturday	Sunday	Notes

week _____

Priorities

-
-
-

Notes
....
....
....
....
....
....
....
....
....

Appointments
_____
_____
_____
_____
_____
_____
_____
_____

Monday

Tuesday

Wednesday

Thursday

Friday

Saturday

Sunday

week _____

Priorities

-
-
-

Notes

....

....

....

....

....

....

Appointments

_____

_____

_____

_____

_____

_____

_____

_____

Monday

Tuesday

Wednesday

Thursday

Friday

Saturday

Sunday

week _____

Priorities

-
-
-

Notes

....
....
....
....
....
....
....
....

Appointments

_____
_____
_____
_____
_____
_____
_____
_____

| Monday |
| Tuesday |
| Wednesday |
| Thursday |
| Friday |
| Saturday |
| Sunday |

week _____

Priorities

-
-
-

Notes

Appointments

| Monday |
| Tuesday |
| Wednesday |
| Thursday |
| Friday |
| Saturday |
| Sunday |

Month of_____

Monday	Tuesday	Wednesday	Thursday

Friday	Saturday	Sunday	Notes

week _____

Priorities

-
-
-

Notes

....
....
....
....
....
....
....

Appointments

_____
_____
_____
_____
_____
_____
_____

Monday

Tuesday

Wednesday

Thursday

Friday

Saturday

Sunday

week _____

Priorities

-
-
-

Notes

Appointments

Monday

Tuesday

Wednesday

Thursday

Friday

Saturday

Sunday

week _____

Priorities

-
-
-

Notes

....
....
....
....
....
....
....

Appointments

_____
_____
_____
_____
_____
_____
_____
_____

| Monday |
| Tuesday |
| Wednesday |
| Thursday |
| Friday |
| Saturday |
| Sunday |

week _____

Priorities

-
-
-

Notes

Appointments

Monday
Tuesday
Wednesday
Thursday
Friday
Saturday
Sunday

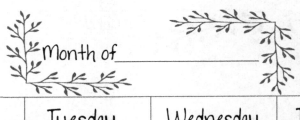

Month of_____

Monday	Tuesday	Wednesday	Thursday

Friday	Saturday	Sunday	Notes

week _____

Priorities

-
-
-

Notes

....
....
....
....
....
....
....
....

Appointments

_____
_____
_____
_____
_____
_____
_____
_____

Monday

Tuesday

Wednesday

Thursday

Friday

Saturday

Sunday

week _____

Priorities

-
-
-

Notes

Appointments

| Monday |
| Tuesday |
| Wednesday |
| Thursday |
| Friday |
| Saturday |
| Sunday |

week _____

Priorities

-
-
-

Notes

....
....
....
....
....
....
....
....

Appointments

_____
_____
_____
_____
_____
_____
_____
_____

Monday

Tuesday

Wednesday

Thursday

Friday

Saturday

Sunday

week _____

Priorities

-
-
-

Notes

Appointments

Monday

Tuesday

Wednesday

Thursday

Friday

Saturday

Sunday

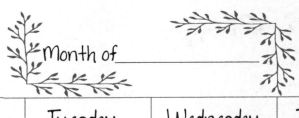

Month of_____

Monday	Tuesday	Wednesday	Thursday

Friday	Saturday	Sunday	Notes

week _____

Priorities

-
-
-

Notes

Appointments

Monday

Tuesday

Wednesday

Thursday

Friday

Saturday

Sunday

week _____

Priorities
-
-
-

Notes
....
....
....
....
....
....
....

Appointments
_____
_____
_____
_____
_____
_____
_____

Monday

Tuesday

Wednesday

Thursday

Friday

Saturday

Sunday

week _____

Priorities

-
-
-

Notes

....
....
....
....
....
....
....
....

Appointments

Monday

Tuesday

Wednesday

Thursday

Friday

Saturday

Sunday

week _____

Priorities

-
-
-

Notes

Appointments

| Monday |
| Tuesday |
| Wednesday |
| Thursday |
| Friday |
| Saturday |
| Sunday |

Month of _____

Monday	Tuesday	Wednesday	Thursday

Friday	Saturday	Sunday	Notes

week _____

Priorities

-
-
-

Notes

....
....
....
....
....
....
....
....

Appointments

_____
_____
_____
_____
_____
_____
_____
_____

Monday

Tuesday

Wednesday

Thursday

Friday

Saturday

Sunday

week _____

Priorities

-
-
-

Notes

....

....

....

....

....

....

....

Appointments

_____

_____

_____

_____

_____

_____

_____

_____

Monday

Tuesday

Wednesday

Thursday

Friday

Saturday

Sunday

week _____

Priorities

-
-
-

Notes

Appointments

| Monday |
| Tuesday |
| Wednesday |
| Thursday |
| Friday |
| Saturday |
| Sunday |

week _____

Priorities

-
-
-

Notes

Appointments

Monday
Tuesday
Wednesday
Thursday
Friday
Saturday
Sunday

vendor contact list

Vendor_____ Phone_____

Email _____

Address_____

_____

Vendor_____ Phone_____

Email _____

Address_____

_____

Vendor_____ Phone_____

Email _____

Address_____

_____

Vendor_____ Phone_____

Email _____

Address_____

_____

Vendor_____ Phone_____

Email _____

Address_____

_____

Vendor_____ Phone_____
Email _____
Address_____

_____

Vendor_____ Phone_____
Email _____
Address_____

_____

Vendor_____ Phone_____
Email _____
Address_____

_____

Vendor_____ Phone_____
Email _____
Address_____

_____

Vendor_____ Phone_____
Email _____
Address_____

_____

Vendor_____ Phone_____
Email _____
Address_____

_____

Vendor_____ Phone_____
Email _____
Address_____
_____

Vendor_____ Phone_____
Email _____
Address_____
_____

Vendor_____ Phone_____
Email _____
Address_____
_____

Vendor_____ Phone_____
Email _____
Address_____
_____

Vendor_____ Phone_____
Email _____
Address_____
_____

Vendor_____ Phone_____
Email _____
Address_____
_____

Vendor_____ Phone_____

Email _____

Address_____

_____

Vendor_____ Phone_____

Email _____

Address_____

_____

Vendor_____ Phone_____

Email _____

Address_____

_____

Vendor_____ Phone_____

Email _____

Address_____

_____

Vendor_____ Phone_____

Email _____

Address_____

_____

Vendor_____ Phone_____

Email _____

Address_____

_____

notes

notes

notes

notes

notes

notes

notes

notes

notes

notes

notes

notes

notes

notes

notes

notes

notes

notes

notes

notes

notes

notes

Made in the USA
Monee, IL
03 January 2022